Heather Hammonds

Contents

Rigby®

A Harcourt Achieve Imprint

www.Rigby.com
1-800-531-5015

Our Fish Tank

We have some fish in our **fish tank**.

We have some plants
in our fish tank, too.

We have rocks
and a little **chest**
in our fish tank.

The plants and the rocks
and the little chest
are for our fish.

Our Fish

Here are my fish.

My fish swim in and out

of the plants.

Here are my sister's fish.

My sister's fish hide

in the plants.

Looking After Our Fish

We look after our fish.

Our fish need:

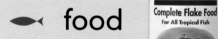 water that is not cold

 food

 plants to hide in

Dad helps us.

Fish Food

Our fish eat fish food.
They eat little water bugs
and worms, too.

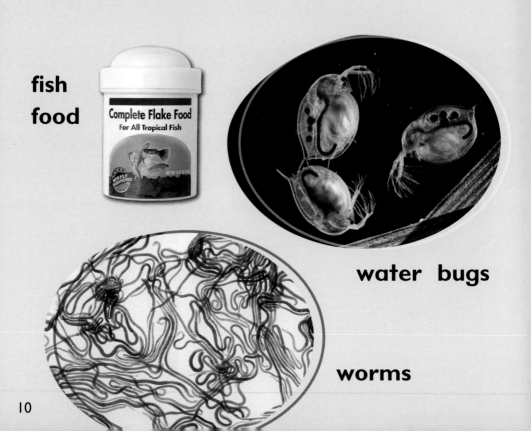

**fish
food**

water bugs

worms

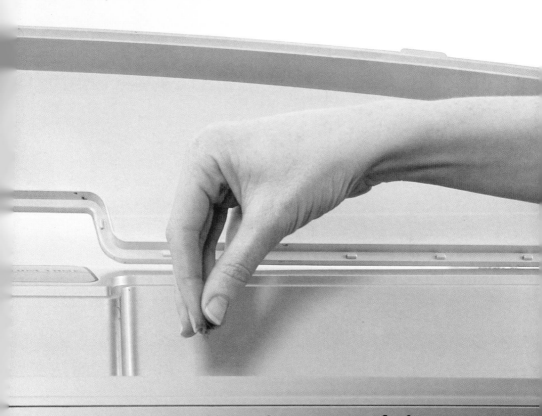

Look at the hungry fish.

New Fish

We are going to get
some new fish.
We see many fish
at this shop.

We see some big fish
and some tiny little fish.

I get an orange fish.

My sister gets

a red and blue fish.

The fish go in bags

of water.

We will carry the bags home.

We like our new fish!

Glossary

chest

fish tank